GRAFFITI

Also by Roger Kilroy & Edward McLachlan

and published by Corgi Books

GRAFFITI 6

Collected and compiled by Roger Kilroy
Wall-to-wall illustrations by
McLACHLAN

CORGI BOOKS

GRAFFITI 6

A CORGI BOOK 0 552 99137 6

First publication in Great Britain

PRINTING HISTORY

Corgi edition published 1985

Corgi Books are published by Transworld Publishers Ltd.,
Century House, 61-63 Uxbridge Road, Ealing, London W5 5SA,
in Australia by Transworld Publishers (Aust.) Pty. Ltd.,
26 Harley Crescent, Condell Park, NSW 2200, and in New
Zealand by Transworld Publishers (N.Z.) Ltd., Cnr. Moselle
and Waipareira Avenues, Henderson, Auckland.

Made and printed in Great Britain by
The Guernsey Press Co. Ltd., Guernsey, Channel Islands.

CONTENTS

(THE IRISH ALPHABET ONLY HAS
20 LETTERS – BECAUSE THE IRISH DON'T
DO ANYTHING AFTER TEA)

A B C D E F G H I J K L M N O P Q R S T

The Tower of Babel was a din of iniquity.

I ALWAYS WANTED TO BE FIRST ON THE LIST BUT I FOUND IT SUCH AARD VARK.

Never hit a man
with glasses.

USE A BRICK!

Mother Nature
is an old cow

BUY A TELESCOPE & SEE URANUS.

NF
NF

No Future
No Freedom
Nasty Fellows
Not Funny

8

I was neutral until a live wire promised me the earth.

FEUDALISM
—it's your count that votes!

OLD AGE IS WHEN YOUR HEIR APPARENT BECOMES A PARENT!

SYNTAX IS ANOTHER NAME FOR CONSCIENCE MONEY

FASHION GOES IN ONE ERA AND OUT THE OTHER.

The Tory Party is the cream of society —thick, rich & full of clots.

ENTRANCE → VIA BACK PASSAGE

WELL, BUGGER-ME!

Some men are wise —some are otherwise

> A MAN WRAPPED UP IN HIMSELF MAKES A **VERY** SMALL PARCEL.

WALLS HAVE EARS

Is that why their ice-cream tastes so bloody awful?

Give me chastity and continence – but not yet.

THE PROBLEM WITH SHORT SKIRTS IS THE UPCREEP

Manslaughter is a terrible thing.

WOMAN'S LAUGHTER IS EVEN WORSE!

13

Christmas is like artificial holly — dead & berried.

BEWARE OF SATAN OR EVIL HAVE HIS WAY

GONE FISSION AT SELLAFIELD

HOPE THE WATER'S NOT TOO ~~NUCLEAR~~ UNCLEAR.

ONE MAN'S FEET ARE ANOTHER MAN'S POISON.

All generalities are untrue.

The start of warm weather is always heralded by the peeling of the belles.

HAY FEVER IS MUCH ATCHOO ABOUT NOTHING.

TO THE CANAL

DRIVER UNDER THE INFLUENCE OF CHILDREN

BIG-BREASTED BLONDES

An old maid is someone who will go so far and no fervour.

SEX IS ALL PROS AND CONS. THE PROS GET ARRESTED, THE CONS GET MARRIED.

A working woman does two jobs for the price of one.

Most women are not
as young as they are painted.

POPULATION EXPLOSIONS ARE
CAUSED BY OVERBEARING WOMEN.

Alice was bad-tempered,
which is why she
threw the looking-glass

AFTER J.

CULTURE CLUB

Today it's Boy George, man!
YESTERDAY IT WAS MAN FRED MANN!

I LIKE COUNTRY MUSIC
most C**ts do!

SYDNEY OPERA HOUSE IS OFF-QUAY

ALLEGRO IS A CHORUS LINE.

Beethoven was so deaf he thought he was a painter.

MACORONI INVENTED THE RADIO

Finnegans Wake is an unfortunate Joyce of book.

The lady cellist was sacked for making her scherzo short

DRINKA PINTA PORTA DAY

TEQUILA IS THE GULP OF MEXICO.

Some drunks have a rye sense of humour.

I never drink unless I'm alone or with someone.

When I'm stoned
I get a little boulder.

DON'T GET A HANGOVER —STAY DRUNK!

The Irish in this bar are all trying to get into the Record Book of Guinnesses!

I thought Genitalia was an Italian airline until I discovered Smirnoff.

I THOUGHT FELLATIO WAS ITALIAN ICE-CREAM UNTIL I DISCOVERED SMIRNOFF.

I thought Smirnoff was just a boring old drink until I discovered sex.

I didn't believe in fairies until I discovered Smirnoff.

TRY VODKA INSTEAD

Begob, Paddy 'Tis the Pope himself

SMIRNOFF

VODKA

Abstinence is thin end of the pledge.

SHE'LL DO ANYTHING FOR A SONG OR A DRINK, SO WE OFFERED A ROUNDELAY.

PEOPLE WHO DRINK BEFORE THEY DRIVE ARE PUTTING THE QUART BEFORE THE HEARSE.

Alcoholics Anonymous?

AA

WUT 173

25

EATING OUT

In an Indian restaurant always eat the curries of your conviction.

NO MAN IS LONELY WHILE EATING SPAGHETTI.

Motorway food isn't my forte.

YOUR EASTER DIET —OVOID CHOCOLATE!

The F-plan Diet is a load of crap!

27

IS oat cuisine another name for porridge?

FAST FOOD HERE

Vienna Rolls

Quiche me quick! GET SICK QUICK!

BUT LONDON SWINGS!

Samovar dishes come from Russia.

BEANS, BEANS,
GOOD FOR THE HEART,
THE MORE YOU EAT,
THE MORE YOU FART.

THE MORE YOU FART,
THE BETTER YOU FEEL,
SO LET'S HAVE BEANS
WITH EVERY MEAL.

I CAME
I SAW
I RAN...QUICKLY
IN THE OPPOSITE DIRECTION.

Tunis or not Tunis: that is the question.

Siamese twins have strong family Thais

In the Middle East things are going from Iraq to ruin.

Soupçon is French for small amount, only morceau

Moroccans leather their kids.

30

ONLY AMERICANS COULD COME UP WITH A GAME CALLED 'CRAP.'

The French have sex, the English have hot-water bottles.

Why don't the Irish see the Eire of their ways?

The Guillotine was a French chopping centre

LEBANON TAKES YOUR BREATH AWAY

The Irish wear two contraceptives to be sure, to be sure.

NORWEGIANS HAVE A TROLL SENSE OF HUMOUR.

BUY in Belfast while shops last.

Gaddaffi, how I Libya, how I Libya

The French call it soixante-neuf
—The Irish call it 96.

I'll be Bejasussed if I'm doin' this another 95 times

33

GAY'S THE WORD

GEORGIE PORGIE
PUDDING AND PIE;
KISSED THE GIRLS
AND MADE THEM CRY.
WHEN THE BOYS
CAME OUT TO PLAY
HE KISSED THEM TOO
—HE'S FUNNY THAT WAY

Gay ghosts give each other the willies.

IS THERE NOBODY QUEER IN BIGGLESWADE?

MORE DEVIATION —LESS POPULATION.

GAY WRAY LOVES KING KONG.

Gays like their vice versa.

THIS YEAR, NOVEMBER FIFTH WILL BE GAY FOLKS' DAY.

GAY DRESSMAKER SEEKS PHALLIC THIMBLE

There's no future in being gay.

Heteros go homo!

Is a puffball a gay dance?

SOME MEN TREAT ALL WOMEN AS SEQUELS.

Shall I compare thee to a summer's day?
COLD, WET & MISERABLE.

37

COURTSHIP IS WHEN YOU TRY EACH OTHER FOR SIGHS

Sarah was just a passing fiancée

It's better to have loved a short man than never to have loved a tall

Free love is bloody expensive these days!

I DISLIKE YOU SOME DAYS, BUT LOVE UNITES.

FAMILIARITY BREEDS CONTEMPT — AND BABIES.

Even though you have a bad code, I still cipher you

Butter
has no
more
calories
than
margarine

WE HAVE
WHEYS OF
MAKING YOU
STORK!

DRINKA
PINTA
MILKA
DAY

stop it
going bad

CANARY FOR SALE PHONE 2637 — going cheep

SING WITH THE CHORAL SOCIETY A choir a good voice

Buy the PENGUIN BOOK OF VERSE I didn't know penguins wrote poetry.

I wandered lonely as a...... snowflake?.... iceberg?..... icefloe?...

Bournemouth
THE LAST RESORT!

Jesus lives!

DOES THAT MEAN EASTER IS CANCELLED FROM NOW ON?

KNIBWORTH VILLAGE Garden Fête

ANOTHER FETE WORSE THAN DEATH

I love life but it's unrequited.

I WAS AN ATHEIST UNTIL I REALISED I WAS GOD.

Banging on walls is for masochists.

EGOTISTS SUFFER FROM I-STRAIN.

45

I CAN'T REMEMBER WHETHER I'VE HAD AMNESIA OR NOT.

The height of insignificance is being none in a million.

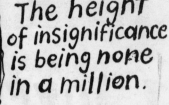

I THINK, THEREFORE I AM,

I AM, THEREFORE I THINK,

I'M PINK, THEREFORE I'M SPAM.

Pessimists look at the world through morose-coloured glasses

Pretentious - Moi?

I'M GOING THROUGH
AN IDENTITY CRISIS
— NORMAN?
— NESTA?
— NAPOLEON!

MY KARMA RAN OVER MY NEIGHBOUR'S DOGMA.

INHIBITIONS MEAN BEING TIED UP IN KNOTS.

The optimist sees the doughnut, the pessimist sees the hole.

REALITY IS AN ILLUSION

God bless atheists!

BUT I'M NOT SO SURE ABOUT AGNOSTICS.

— GOD

48

KNOBS AND KNOCKERS

FEMINISTS SHOULD BE
BEHIND BRAS.

Is an Irishman's called an O'Toole?

Penis envy is a phallusy!

ITS 12 INCHES LONG BUT I DON'T USE IT AS A RULE.

COQ AU VIN = BREWER'S DROOP

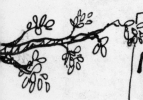

> A SHILLELAGH IS A LARGE WOODEN ONE WITH KNOBBLY BITS.

Women runners are a lot of jogglers.

LOOS LIVING

GIPSIES DON'T NEED CONTRACEPTIVES AS THEY HAVE CRYSTAL BALLS AND CAN SEE THEMSELVES COMING!

SUREX

LOVE'S LABOURS LOST

SUBJECT TO VAT IF USED ON PREMISES

Rubbergard

BUY one and avoid the issue

BEWARE OF REMOULDS

↑ THESE MACHINES ARE RUSTY AND ROTTING SO WHAT MUST THE CONTENTS BE LIKE!?!

Don't worry
about the
menopause
- worry about
the men who
don't !

STAY OFF THE PILL
AND LET NATURE
TAKE ITS CURSE.

My wife ran off
with a Swiss,
WHAT?- YOUR OLD LADEE TOO!

54

MARRIAGE ON THE ROCKS

A wedding is a funeral where you can smell your own flowers.

A HAPPY MARRIAGE IS A QUESTION OF MIND OVER MATTER

-I don't mind and you don't matter!

A bachelor is an unaltared male

A bachelor never Mrs anyone.

Alimony is paying for something you don't get.

PRIESTS CAN'T MARRY WITHOUT PRIOR APPROVAL.

Divorcees get richer by degrees.

POP YOUR BODY!

POP OUGHT TO KNOW WHOSE BODY HE'S GOT!

57

THE ETERNAL TRIANGLE IS USUALLY RIGHT TANGLED.

one good turn.... gives you all the blankets.

Miserable Bastards!

SUNDAY 16 JUNE Father's Day

FATHER'S DAY IS LIKE MOTHER'S DAY BUT YOU DON'T NEED TO SPEND AS MUCH

58

NOTHING BUT THE TRUTH

MONEY TALKS!
Mine always says, 'Goodbye'

MONEY DOESN'T TALK, IT SWEARS!

Money talks but its recently sent me to Coventry.

MONEY IS LIKE MUCK— ONLY USEFUL WHEN ITS SPREAD AROUND.

TAKE CARE OF THE PENCE AND THE INLAND REVENUE WILL TAKE CARE OF THE REST

The trouble with the world is the copulation explosion.

MUM'S THE WORD
—not if you use contraceptives.

Tell it not in Gath
—THAY IT IN ELECTRITHITY INTHTEAD!

Graffiti is squatters writes.

In nuclear warfare all men are cremated equal.
Byegones be byegones, Konstantin, old pal?...

LORD, GIVE ME PATIENCE - NOW!

THE HARDEST PART OF BEING DOWN AND OUT IS WATCHING THE WORLD GO BUY.

Enough is <u>never</u> enough!

THE RIOTING'S ON THE WALL.

Live within your income even if you have to borrow to do so!

I'M GOING TO RUN AWAY FROM HOME AS SOON AS WE GET ONE.

I love London but it's over-rated!

Old age is 15 years older than you are.

UNEMPLOYMENT ISN'T WORKING

JUDGES DO IT IN WIGS.
Solicitors do it in lawsuits
Organic gardeners do it with compost.

UNIVERSITY LECTURERS
DO IT BY DEGREES.

Architects do it in style.

Miners do it in pits.

NORMAN TEBBIT DOES IT ON SPITE

Bricklayers do it with erections
—But not for long...

PAVAROTTI DOES IT ON SONG.

Torvill and Dean do it on thin ice.

Kinnock does it in opposition to Thatcher.

MONKS DO IT HABITUALLY

SOCCER HOOLIGANS DO IT IN.

POTTERS DO IT ON A WHEEL.

Conductors do it
with a baton.

CARPENTERS DO IT
AGAINST THE GRAIN.

Doctors do it
on call

DANCERS DO IT
ON POINTS.

Shepherds do it
in flocks

FLORISTS DO IT
IN BUNCHES

Train drivers do it
on flexible rostering.

Farmers do it
with the CAP

GLAZIERS DO IT IN PANE.

QCs do it
in chambers

PEOPLE POWER

OEDIPUS WAS A NERVOUS REX

An adman writes the prose, and cons.

THE 3 MUSKETEERS WERE PRETTY FENCY FELLOWS

IS MICHAEL FOOT A LEG-END?

Mickey Mouse was a rat!

A PURITAN NOES WHAT HE LIKES

SHOPLIFTERS HAVE THE GIFT OF THE GRAB.

Samson loved Delilah, until she bald him out.

Flash Gordon invented the zip.

KING MIDAS HAD A GILT COMPLEX

THE UPPER CRUST ARE JUST A LOT OF CRUMBS STICKING TOGETHER

Napoleon wore his sleeve on his heart.

Organic gardeners till it like it is.

PEDAGOGUES GET EXCITED OVER FEET.

Frankenstein was a lonely man until he discovered how to make friends.

Skinheads have more hair than brains.

MAURICE, A MINER, WAS A BULL-NOSED CHAP FROM OXFORD.

Lady Chatterley's gardener was a bit rough around the hedges

But amazing in the maze!!

SHERLOCK HOLMES WAS JUST AN OLD CLUE SNIFFER

Dracula loved in vein.

J. R. APPEARS UNDER AN ASSUMED NAME.

Adam was Eve's mother

QUESTIONS, QUESTIONS

DOES POPEYE STUFF OLIVE?

Where's your erogenous zone?

BETWEEN PUTNEY BRIDGE
AND FULHAM BROADWAY.

What's green and rolls about the garden?
— A ruptured leprechaun.

HOW COME THERE'S ONLY ONE MONOPOLIES COMMISSION?

Is this a dago which I see before me?

Is copper nitrate policemen's overtime?

Are you pregnant?

IF YOU DON'T LIKE IT YOU CAN LUMP IT!

Is a gynaecologist's consulting room just a cervix station?

DO GOVERNMENT ARTISTS DRAW THE DOLE?

WHAT ABOUT RED CHINA? Looks ever so nice on a white tablecloth!

RUGBY PLAYERS NEED LEATHER BALLS

Rugby is a game played by men with oval balls.

SHOW US YOUR CHEEK, ARSENAL

Cricket players are only as young as they field

A cricket player is just a jack-in-a-box

Skiers often jump to contusions.

PARACHUTISTS JUMP TO CONCLUSIONS!

Pontoon is a form of bridge

I GET WHIST OFF WITH CARDS

Wrestling is the sport of clings.

MONOPOLY MAKES ME BOARD

FISHING IS A MATTER OF BAIT AND SEA

SMOKE GETS IN YOUR EYES

SMOKE- CHOKE- CROAK!

CANCER CURES SMOKING

Death cures cancer!

Does passive smoking give you cancer quietly?

Will no smoking on the Tube mean fewer Pullmanry complaints?

IF YOU CLIMB TO THE TOP OF VESUVIUS YOU CAN SEE THE CREATOR SMOKING

TRANSPORTS OF DELIGHT

Its a Goodyear for worn tyres.

BUY A NEW CAR

I don't have the motorvation.

AND I CAN'T A-FORD ONE

and I have the same old Saab story

BESIDES, THEY DON'T MAKE CARS LIKE THEY AUTO.

There are only two kinds of pedestrians
— the quick and the dead

German cars are very good on Benz.

WHAT'S DAT CAR, DAD?
DAT, SON, IS A JAPANESE CAR.

TRAVEL BROADENS THE MIND
IS THAT WHY AIRLINE PILOTS ARE FATHEADS?

When she drives and he's in the passenger seat, its a kind of duel control.

Its takes a lot of bread to own a Rolls.

SPAGHETTI JUNCTION IS A SITE FOR SORE EYES.

JOIN
The Guards

← and get a free hair transplant

I GOT THESE FOR FAINTING THREE TIMES IN FRONT OF THE QUEEN.

Swine!
She probably
wanted to
faint first.

The Army will
make you a man!

I'd like a great big
butch he-man!
WOULD YOU CONTEMPLATE
A NAVAL TYPE?

92

What about the Gurkhas?

FREEDOM FOR THE GURKHING CLASSES!

$$\frac{WREN}{SEXED} + AB = \frac{AB}{WREN}$$

$$\frac{AB}{SEAS} + \frac{WREN}{DUE} = \frac{WREN}{WROUGHT}$$

$$AB - £200 = WREN^2$$

Battledress is just a tog-of-war.

Join the Navy
and see the world

SAILORS ALWAYS MAKE SURE THERE'S A PORT IN EVERY WIFE!

4/5 of it is covered by water anyway!

All the nice girls love a sailor.

THE TROUBLE IS NICE SAILORS ONLY LOVE EACH OTHER.

VICE IS NICE

Prostitutes are not
really lost women
— they're just mislaid.

PORNOGRAPHERS
OFFER A VICE
TO THE LOVE-LORN.

TEMPORARY ERECTIONS
DEMOLISHED — Phone Bayswater 256

VIRTUE IS ITS
OWN REWARD
NOT ROUND SOHO IT ISN'T!!

A little weed never did Bill & Ben any harm

DON'T DRINK AND DRIVE HOME —SMOKE AND FLY HOME!

Glue sniffers suffer from gluecinations

GLUE SNIFFERS ARE A STUCK-UP LOT

It's Sellotape —one has to start somewhere.

WORKERS RULE

What have the bosses got that we haven't?

LARGE SALARIES, COMPANY CARS AND EXPENSE ACCOUNTS!

A large company is like a septic tank — All the really big chunks float to the top.

LAUGH, AND THE WORLD LAUGHS WITH YOU. WORK, AND YOU WORK ALONE.

Nothing is impossible to those who don't have to do it themselves.

If I didn't have to work so hard I'd have more time to feel depressed.

AUDIO TYPISTS HAVE TO TAKE A LOT FOR GRUNTED

Time is money — IS THAT WHY I'M ALWAYS LATE?

99

This company is full
of willing people
— Those who are willing to work
and those who are willing to let 'em.

I'D ENJOY THE DAY MORE IF
IT STARTED LATER.

Procrastination will
rule one day, OK?

THINK AHEA
D

Don't work
— there's too
much to do!

I'M GIVING UP WORK AND LEARNING TO STEAL — A CAT BURGLAR IS TEACHING MIAOW.

careful, wibley, they're suede

A yes-man stoops to concur

SEX CERTIFICATE

Virginity is like a bubble
— one prick and it's gone

DOUBLE YOUR CHANCES
— BE BI-SEXUAL

VD is just a clap
on the back
YOU'VE BEEN DOING
IT THE WRONG WAY
ROUND, DEARIE.

THE PEDESTAL

A little coitus Never hoitus

There's a vas deferens between the male and female genital organs

MEN WHO PUT WOMEN ON PEDESTALS RARELY KNOCK THEM OFF!

USE CONTRACEPTIVES
ON EVERY CONCEIVABLE
OCCASION!

Advice to
would-be cloners:
Go f**k yourself!

PETTING IS THE STUDY OF ANATOMY IN BRAILLE

AN ERECTION IS LIKE
THE THEORY OF RELATIVITY.
—THE MORE YOU THINK
ABOUT IT THE HARDER IT GETS.

Incest is the theory of relativity

Is oral contraception when you talk your way out of it.

Castration is a eunuch experience

A HARD MAN IS GOOD TO FIND.

An absolute cat-astrophe!

For a meeting
of the sexes
you need agenda

Men are either
f******s or wankers!

What I'd like is sex of one kind
and half a dozen of the other!

DON'T WAIT
MORE THAN
A COUPLE
OF SEX
FOR A
HERMAPHRODITE

Unless you're
a bloody
snail that is!

YOUTH IS WASTED
ON THE YOUNG

Yesterday I couldn't
spell 'educated'
– Now I are it.

ST. CUTHBERT'S
SCHOOL
FOR BOYS

Herod was right!

I WENT HOME LAST NIGHT
BUT MY PARENTS HAD
MOVED HOUSE.

MATRICULATION MAKES YOU BLIND.

Fractions are often vulgar.

Hastings 1066 was William the Conqueror's phone number.

I have an above average QI.

PUBERTY IS A HAIR-RAISING EXPERIENCE

SEE my PUBERTY 5p a Look Q·HERE

cross-eyed, teachers can't control their pupils.

BETWEEN YOUR EYES IS SOMETHING THAT SMELLS.

OXFORD NEEDS GENTLEMEN AND SCULLERS

STOP FRENCH TESTS!

and cricket tests!

AND SPELING TESTS!

ZOO TIME

BRITAIN'S RIVERS ARE GETTING CLEANER
Happy dace are here again!

IF YOU TREAD ON A CAT'S TAIL ARE ITS FELINES HURT?

A bird in the hand... Does it on your wrist.

CRAP!

The pious bird with the scarlet breast, our little English robin

William Wordsworth

Love me, love my dog!

I WOULD, BUT IT'S AGAINST THE LAW.

CATTLE SHOWS ARE UDDER CHAOS

Tiger! Tiger! burning bright. Who has set your tail alight?

KEEPING DOGS IN THE CITY MEANS THE STREETS ARE ALWAYS FULL OF OLD FAMILIAR FAECES